Drawing
AN ARTIST'S FIRST STEP

Drawing
AN ARTIST'S FIRST STEP

igloo

Published by Igloo Books Limited
Henson Way
Telford Way Industrial Estate
Kettering
Northants
NN16 8PX
info@igloo-books.com

This edition published 2005

ISBN 1-84561-228-0

Project management: Kandour Ltd

Editorial and design management: Emma Hayley and Jenny Ross
Co-ordinator: Adam Phillips
Author and Illustrator: Sarah Green
Cover and text design: Paul Barton
Layout: Kurt Young
Additional illustrations: Peter J Green (John) and Carolyn Green
Photography: Daley Rowner, Derwent, Photos.com
With thanks to Victoria Chow

Contents

An Introduction to Drawing

An Artist's First Step

Learning to draw is a very rewarding experience. You will be able to capture moments forever, express thoughts and feelings, and learn to become more observant about the world that surrounds you.

Most of us have some experience of art, normally from formal education. Once we leave school, we tend to leave any practice of art behind too. If you have ever wondered if you really could learn to draw, or rediscover any childhood talent, then this book is for you. It will guide you gently through all the main elements that any budding artist needs to create successful compositions. There will be simple-to-follow exercises which will teach basic rules of composition and perspective, as well as how to tackle specific subjects, such as landscapes and portraits.

The emphasis will be on learning to master basic techniques in pencil drawing, as well as guidance on how to apply color using different drawing mediums.

You will learn how to use a sketchbook to collect ideas and inspiration for pictures, as well as act as a practicing tool. All the exercises will gradually build your confidence to allow you to develop your own style and get creating beautiful pictures. There will be lots of tips on how to begin mastering simple techniques that, over time and with practice, will give you excellent foundation drawing skills. Above all, you will have fun and learn new skills which will give you a lifetime of pleasure.

- Follow the step-by-step examples of methods and techniques that will help develop confidence and ability.

- Learn how to use a sketchbook to practice techniques, collect reference material, and begin creating original compositions.

- Discover how to use different drawing materials to create a range of textures and tonal qualities which will add perspective and atmosphere to any drawing.

- Understand the importance of careful planning when creating a composition by using a simple checklist.

- Begin to master perspective and proportion to create the illusion of three-dimensional space within a composition.

- Learn about the range of drawing materials and equipment that are available and how to select the most appropriate for your needs.

Rediscover the joys of drawing and learn how to make the most of your creativity

Why Learn to Draw?

Learning to draw can seem a daunting prospect as there are so many different things to think about before you even put pencil to paper. However, everyone has the physical ability to be able to draw—children will automatically make marks on paper and begin to express themselves and the world that surrounds them long before they can write.

Drawings have been found in prehistoric caves which were used as a rudimentary form of communication long before language and writing came about. Drawing is one of the fundamental things that humans use to convey emotion and capture a sense of time.

A drawing can be as simple as a series of marks on any surface that conveys some kind of message or emotion, or an incredibly technically complicated, emotionally expressive statement.

Drawings have many functions and can be made in limitless ways–the only restriction is the artist's imagination. A drawing can be made from a pencil

on paper, but it can also be created from other mediums, even paint. There is a crossover between the two disciplines of drawing and painting–in fact it is virtually impossible to paint without having drawing skills. Many other craft-based techniques rely on a simple grasp of drawing in one way or another draughtsmen, architects and designers all need to draw when developing concepts. Even computers use basic drawing principles in many graphic-based disciplines such as layout and web-site design.

- It is important to learn how to judge when a drawing is complete. Many people find drawing a challenge because they believe they have to produce a direct representation of whatever it is they are looking at but, in most cases, a good drawing is as much about what is left out as to that which is captured on the paper. A good artist will learn, often through trial and error, just what can be left out to create a visually stimulating piece. There is nothing to prevent an artist from interpreting a scene in any way that they feel will benefit the overall composition.

This book will help you to interpret any subject in a spontaneous and fresh way, which will give feeling and meaning to your drawings.

Drawing does not have to produce a direct representation of what you see—through trial and error, you will find a style that works for you

Defining Drawing

Remember, a drawing is a series of marks that convey emotions and meanings. A good drawing is one that works on this level, as opposed to a technically superior composition that lacks depth and understanding of the subject.

After all, a drawing is an interpretation of the subject as the artist views it. Each artist will, through practice, begin to develop a feeling of individuality as they discover their own style.

Some people draw because it is the beginning of a longer process—for example, when composing a painting. Yet drawing is an art form in its own right. There are many artists who choose drawing as their main type of creative expression. Either way, there are certain things to consider before you begin. If you decide to make an objective drawing then you will be looking to create a representational, or "life-like," composition. This will create a fairly accurate, factually informative piece of work. A subjective drawing will be far more expressive, with more passion and feeling, which may even result in a very abstract composition.

Most good artists are able to find a balance between these two types of drawing. There will be times when an objective approach is the best option, especially if it is to record certain details of a time and a place, or as a reference, such as when planning a painting or other type of art form. This does not mean that there should be no hint of expression as even an objective composition needs to have life and feeling within it to be engaging. At other times, a subjective, free-flowing drawing may

still rely on some objective elements to make sure that the work can be easily interpreted.

Another consideration is what type of drawing medium should be used for each kind of drawing. Much of this will be determined by the effect that you wish to create, although some types of drawing material will be harder to use in certain situations. This will be one of the things that will come with practice. You will understand through trial and error which materials work best. By the end of this book, you will have a clear understanding of the types of materials available and which are the best methods of applying them to your drawing.

If you feel inspired by a subject, then you are halfway to creating a successful composition. Most drawings work because the artist has been able to connect with the subject. You may have a favorite subject that you wish to concentrate on, such as landscape painting or still life flowers. It is worth attempting other styles and mediums from time to time as this will prevent you from becoming stale and may even give a fresh perspective on your favorite subject. Trying new things can be daunting, but challenging yourself as an artist is exciting and you may discover that you have talents that you never thought were there.

There is no such thing as a right way to draw; rather there are techniques that can be used to help you gain confidence as an artist, and even these can be manipulated to create new visual effects as your confidence grows.

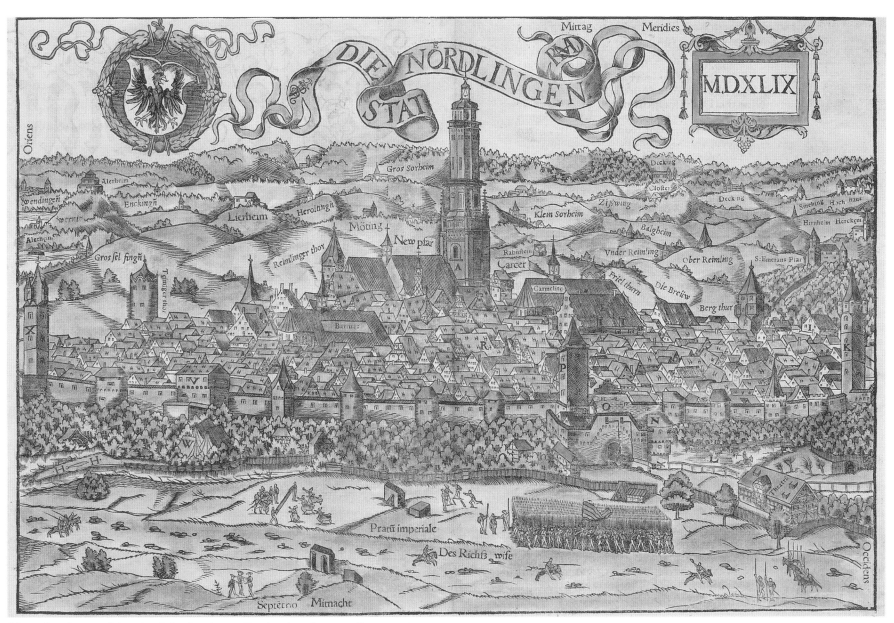

Mastering the art of drawing is both a demanding but hugely rewarding pursuit

Introduction to Planning your Drawing

For the beginner, it can be frustrating to see how some people can seemingly pick up a pencil and create a work of art with hardly any effort. A blank piece of paper appears to hold no fear for them as they dash off a brilliant drawing.

While these types of artists seem to have a natural talent, it does not mean that they are not making a series of decisions about their drawing before and while they create it. It is just that they are so comfortable with the process that it seems that they are doing very little.

Any artist should have a mental checklist that they go through before embarking on a drawing. Careful planning will mean that you are more likely to produce a piece of work that is satisfying and does what you set out to achieve. Depending on the type of drawing you require, you will need to decide on a range of factors which will influence the end result; subject matter, timescale and materials are all crucial things to consider during the initial planning stage.

Things to think about when planning a drawing

- What do you want your drawing to "say?" What visual impact do you want your drawing to have and how do you hope to achieve it? Decide on an objective or subjective approach. Is your drawing for research? If so, an objective view point is best. If you want to portray emotion or the feel of a specific place, object or event, then be more subjective.

- What will be the best drawing medium to achieve the effect you want? Think about the practicalities, such as: will the drawing be done on location? What level of detail will your drawing contain? Certain types of drawing medium will be more suited to finer detail, such as pencils and pens, whereas charcoal, pastels, and chalk will give a more fluid, expressive feeling and can quickly capture the essence of a subject–all these will be described in more detail in the "materials and equipment" section of this book.

- Have you done sufficient research? Are you working from memory or photographs, or are you on location? If you are collecting data for a composition then how will you record all the relevant information? Will you be using a sketchbook? Perhaps you need to make additional notes or do several sketches from different viewpoints. Maybe you should do a range of drawings; some subjective, to capture the mood; others more objective, to ensure you include all the relevant details you require for any final composition–you will learn how to create and use a sketchbook later in this book.

- How are you going to apply the image to the paper? Will you be working in "landscape" or "portrait?" What viewpoint will you be taking? All these questions will be dealt with in the next section of the book.

As you become more confident with drawing, you will find that these types of considerations will become second nature to you. Don't worry if you make a few mistakes along the way, or forget to do certain things. You will always learn from anything that goes wrong–in fact, you may even achieve some fantastic results by attempting to experiment a little.

Creating your composition

What makes a good composition? It can be hard to say exactly why we think one drawing is better composed than another–often it is just because it "feels" right. As you get more experienced at creating your own, you will begin to recognize those elements that can really improve a drawing.

Composition is the way in which an artist designs and organizes a picture in relation to the space available. It should be determined by the elements that you want your picture to include mood, atmosphere, and impact, as well as the actual subject matter.

If a drawing is well-composed, then it will invite the eye in and allow it to eventually rest in the center of the composition, after having taken in the whole picture. The edges of the picture act as the frame, so it is important not to over-emphasize the outer area as this will distract from the rest of the composition.

- An important consideration is the use of space within a composition. Each object and space within a picture bear a direct relation to each other—these are called "positive" and "negative" spaces. For example, in a landscape, the positive space would be the objects: trees, hills, buildings, clouds, etc. The negative space is the areas between the objects. If these elements are successfully interwoven, then the composition will be successful.

- Using contrast also improves a composition. For example, to emphasize how dominant something is, place a small object next to it—light/dark; thick/thin; shadow/light.

- Keep your picture balanced—if you draw attention to one side then the rhythm of the picture will be distorted and it will appear unbalanced. Always try to keep the eye stimulated enough to explore the picture, without it becoming distracted.

Composition is the foundation of any good drawing

- Think of an element within the whole composition which will act as the focal point– something for the eye to finally be drawn to. This will normally be of some significance to the picture as a whole; perhaps this object or person will help the artist to reflect the meaning of the piece. Remember not to place it too centrally as the eye will naturally go direct to that point. Instead, try leading the eye around the picture by making the composition as interesting as possible.

- Don't place objects in rows as this could make your picture appear lifeless and boring. Vary the viewpoint to create more movement around the picture and give it greater depth.

The Golden Mean

Most drawings and paintings are done on rectangular paper or canvas. As a general rule, landscape (including skyscape, seascape, and townscape) compositions are created with the long edge of the paper or canvas as the horizontal line, whereas portrait compositions use the long edge as the vertical as this best suits the shape of the human body and face. However, as with everything in art, you are at liberty to experiment with these norms.

It is not advisable to place objects within a picture too close to the center of a composition, or split it centrally, either vertically or horizontally, as this will lead the eye directly to the mid point and the rest of the picture will be lost.

When using these rectangular, horizontal or vertical canvases, the usual rule is that you apply the Golden Mean or Golden Ratio principle when composing the layout of your picture. This means dividing up a rectangle using geometry which was devised by Renaissance painters, who believed it was the most perfect layout.

It is based on the mathematical relationship between three points on a straight line in which the ratio AC:BC equals the ratio BC:AC. If that sounds confusing, a simpler way of describing it is that any picture should be divided up by a ratio of 2:3. In other words, an important aspect of the composition should be placed about two-thirds of the way across the paper to create a harmonious picture. This can be on the vertical or horizontal lines, so is appropriate for landscape and portrait viewpoints.

Using a viewfinder

To make composing a picture easier, try making a portable viewfinder. Use a fairly thick piece of card, about 4in x 5$\frac{1}{2}$in. Cut a rectangle of 1in x 1$\frac{1}{2}$in from the middle of the sheet. Hold it away from you, shutting one eye, and look at the composition. Use this to "frame" your subject to decide the best viewpoint to begin drawing from.

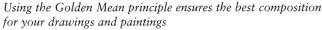

Using the Golden Mean principle ensures the best composition for your drawings and paintings

15

Although it takes time to master, perspective will boost the realism of your pictures

The basics of perspective

Perspective in a drawing is what gives it its sense of depth. Imagine the drawing of a long straight road. If you were standing looking directly up it, the lines which mark the edges of the road would seem to converge as they fade away into the distance. The point at which these two lines meet is known as the vanishing point.

Of course, we know that these lines are in fact parallel and do not actually converge at all. However, this optical illusion gives an immediate sense of distance. Artists use this optical trick to give their work a sense of realism. It looks incredibly complicated, but the effect of perspective is fairly easy to achieve and, as with most technical areas of drawing, will become easier the more often you practice it.

The main elements of perspective

The horizon line

This is a horizontal line which is roughly level with the observer's eyes. If the observer changes position, such as when sitting or standing, so too does the horizon line.

The point of view

This is the direction in which the observer is looking.

The vanishing point

A composition that uses perspective will have at least one vanishing point, which is usually situated on the horizon line. There are three types of vanishing point: parallel perspective, oblique perspective and aerial perspective. These types of perspective are directly related to the number of vanishing points within the composition.

Parallel perspective: this is when all the parallel lines appear to converge to one point in the picture.

Oblique perspective: this is when there are two vanishing points, at different points of view along the horizon line. The horizontal parallel lines recede toward the horizon and form two converging sets of lines which meet at their respective vanishing points.

Aerial perspective: this is slightly different to either parallel or oblique perspective, as the vanishing point is above or below the horizon line. Often aerial perspective will be used alongside oblique perspective, which gives the subject of a composition a feeling of height or depth.

Parallel perspective—simple exercises

Parallel or "one-point" perspective is the easiest type of perspective to draw as there is only one vanishing point. Look at how the box in the illustration is drawn so that all the parallel lines converge as they move into the distance.

- Try drawing a similar box several times, altering its width and height.

- Once you feel comfortable doing that, see if you can attempt the room shown in the two remaining illustrations. It is guided by exactly the same rules. Only the parallel lines that recede are affected, while the horizontal and vertical lines, which are parallel to the paper's edges, remain unaffected.

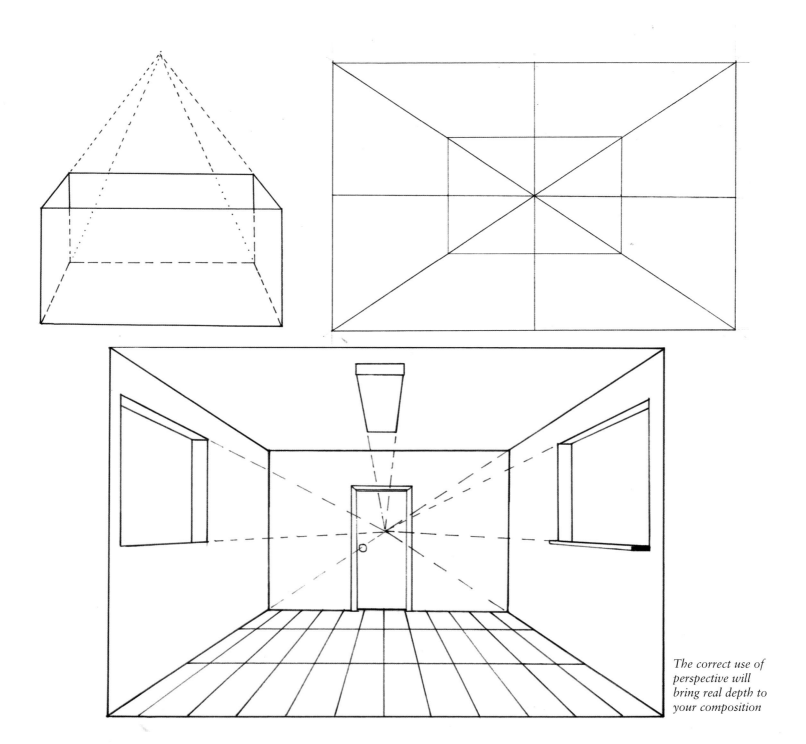

The correct use of perspective will bring real depth to your composition

Planning your Drawing

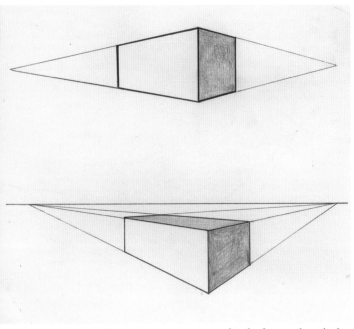

Artists use perspective as a kind of optical trick that helps pull the viewer into the picture

Oblique perspective—simple exercises

If you are using an oblique, or "two-point," perspective you can create compositions which have subjects placed at an angle. This is very useful when drawing buildings, as often they are placed at different angles in relation to each other.

- Use a box similar to that in your first perspective exercise. Place two vanishing points on either side of your horizon line and use them to create your guide lines. The lines should converge at the front edge of the box.

You can even alter the viewpoint of an object using oblique perspective: distant, close-up, "bird's-eye," and "worm's-eye" view. Try the following exercises:

- If the box is viewed from a distance, the box appears smaller with little distortion of the sides, which slope back at less of an angle than a box which is closer.

- If the vanishing points are close to the subject on a normal horizon line, you will get the effect of an object which is very close to you. This is called "foreshortening." The sides of the box seem quite distorted.

- A low or "worm's-eye" viewpoint means that the horizon line moves down the box. This makes any converging lines of perspective above the horizon line appear steeper.

- A "bird's-eye" viewpoint is created by moving the horizon line upwards, which gives an effect of looking down onto the subject.

- By adding a third or "aerial" vanishing point, you can give a further feeling of height to a composition. This works especially well when drawing tall buildings.

Other ways of giving a sense of perspective

You can also give a sense of perspective within a composition by using tone and color. These will be discussed in more detail later in the book.

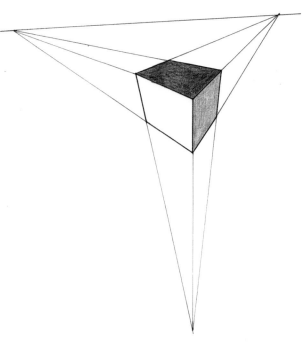

While you should never blame your tools for a job done badly, it is essential to have the right equipment to help create the best end result. Follow this practical guide and you will have the perfect companion to accompany you on your first steps as an artist.

Selecting the Best Tools

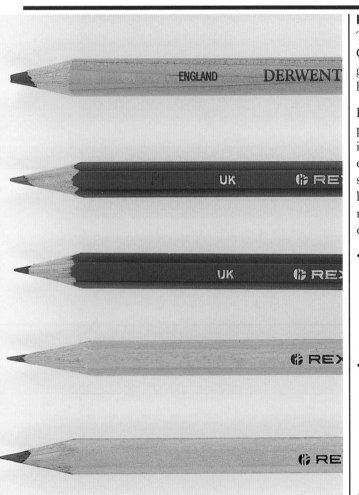

Pencils

The most common drawing material is the pencil. Often called a "lead pencil," it is actually made of graphite and comes in many different degrees of hardness. These range from 9H to 8B.

Pencils are incredibly versatile and are the most popular medium to use when drawing and sketching. They are portable and mistakes can easily be erased. They are also very cheap and can make a seemingly endless array of marks. Pencils may seem less glamorous than some of the other drawing materials available, but for sheer versatility and ease of use, the humble pencil cannot be beaten.

- H indicates "hard" when grading pencils. H pencils are best suited for technical drawings, as they are harder to use due to the marks they make. They will indent paper easily and are hard to erase, making mistakes difficult to remove. They are also less fluid that the softer B pencils.

- B indicates "soft," meaning that the marks on the paper are darker, softer and wider than those of a harder H pencil. It is the B selection of pencils that most artists will use when drawing. They are much easier to manipulate and can be erased easily, as well as smudged and blended to make a range of tonal and textural effects.

Always use a good quality pencil as poor examples will give an uneven mark and may damage your drawing surface. There are some excellent tins available which contain the full range of artists' graphite pencils. You can experiment with all the different gradings, replacing individual pencils as you use them up. Some pencils will make different graded effects, according to the brand, so once you find a pencil you like, stick to that manufacturer so you will always know what you are getting.

You may find that at times you will need a harder pencil for very detailed compositions. A good range of pencils will include a 2H pencil for precise drawing; an HB for basic note-taking and quick sketches; a 2B for most sketching tasks, and a 4B and 6B for heavier shading and tonal work.

There are other drawing materials that are considered similar to the common pencil. These include:

- Pure graphite sticks: use as you would a normal pencil. These are sticks of pure graphite, encased in a thin film of plastic, which make wide strokes when used on the angle.

- Sepia sketching pencil: this is a brown pigmented pencil which was traditionally used when sketching a subject onto a canvas for painting. Used on its own, it produces a pale brown line which is smudgable and water soluble. It is a type of chalk.

- Sanguine sketching pencil: this gives a richer brown color and is also used to sketch onto a canvas. It is often used alongside white chalk on colored paper.

- White sketching pencil: this can be used as a highlighter with pencil, charcoal or chalk, or on its own on colored paper.

Colored pencils

Colored pencils are similar to graphite pencils. The color is made by mixing pigment, clay and wax. The softness of the pencil is determined by the amount of wax.

You can create all sorts of effects with colored pencils, including overlaying different colors, although they cannot be mixed together in the way paint can. This means that there are hundreds of different color variations available to give you as much choice as possible. Because you do not have to mix the colors yourself, they are a good way of beginning to explore colored compositions.

Some colored pencils are also water-soluble, which gives the added benefit of being able to add water to create an effect like watercolor paints. The pencil color is applied to the paper as normal, and then water is applied with a brush which mixes the colored pigments together as a "wash." This gives a pale, delicate feel to a drawing and can be used throughout the entire composition or as highlights.

Charcoal

One of the first drawing materials ever used were pieces of charred wood from the fires of prehistoric man. This ancient drawing tool is still used today in the form of charcoal. It is made from willow sticks, which are prepared in kilns.

Charcoal is incredibly easy to use and can make loads of different marks and tonal effects. It is not really appropriate for fine detailed work but is excellent for producing free-flowing, expressive compositions.

Charcoal needs to be "fixed" once the drawing is completed to prevent smudging. There are lots of different fixative sprays available for this.

There are many types of charcoal available: pencils, compressed sticks and twigs.

- Stick charcoal is made from kiln-fired willow twigs and comes in many grades of thickness. They are the most natural form of charcoal. They are more breakable than the other forms of charcoal available but their delicate structure means that the smaller sticks can produce some quite fine detail.

- Compressed charcoal is easier to use as the charcoal powder is mixed with a binder to make a thicker stick which is harder to break. Consequently, it is less effective for fine detail but can fill in large areas of tone quickly.

- Charcoal pencils can be used as you would a normal pencil but give the effect of charcoal. They are cleaner to use and can create detailed compositions as they can be sharpened, but they are less spontaneous than charcoal sticks.

- Use white chalk as a highlighter when drawing with charcoal for a dramatic contrast.

Drawing Equipment and Materials

Pastels and crayons

There are two main types of pastel–hard and soft. They produce quite different effects and can be purchased in many colors. They are made by combining pigment, chalk and gum. Soft pastels have a very particular bloom, which is velvet-like, with rich tones that can be blended together to create very delicate effects. Hard pastels contain more binder and so are less vibrant, although they are easy to handle and can be used to add detail and fine lines to a composition. They can also be purchased in pencil form. Pastels can be rubbed away with a clean rag or a finger. Any finished piece should always be fixed using a spray varnish.

- Oil pastels give an effect similar to oil paint with their rich, thick pigments. They are very moist and give a painterly feel to a composition. They are soft and can be applied light over dark, which is useful as mistakes are hard to remove. The best way is to scrape excess oil pastel away with a sharp craft knife or fingernail, then reapply color over the top.

- Wax crayons are similar to oil pastels. They are an ancient medium and were common in Egyptian times. They are greasier than oil pastels and if layered, produce an impermeable, smooth finish. It is difficult to use lighter colors over dark wax crayons, so colors need to be carefully planned. If mistakes are made, a sharp knife can scrape away excess wax. This can be used as a technique to allow lighter colors to be highlighted through the darker ones. Wax crayons do not need fixing.

- Conte crayons are very compressed chalks which are harder than pastels. They are available in a range of muted colors and are traditionally used for creating tonal studies. Conte crayons do not need fixing.

Pens and markers

The first basic pens were simply sticks dipped into ink. Then feather quill pens were created which allowed for a more constant, fluid line. Nowadays, there are hundreds of different pens of various thicknesses, color and permanency. Some should be used with dipping ink or cartridges, whereas others have their own inbuilt supply. They are all capable of creating interesting lines and textures.

- Some pens can be used with water to create a wash, similar to the principle behind watercolor painting. This technique softens lines and blocks in subtle areas of tone. Ink can also be spattered, blobbed, stippled and sponged to great effect. These techniques will be described in more detail throughout the book.

- Marker pens give a variety of lines and colors and can be blended by overlaying darker tones over light. The ink is translucent and can cover a large area of paper quickly, giving any composition a very immediate, fresh feel. The larger nibbed varieties make a range of interesting lines and can fill in blocks of color with ease. There are a huge number of ink types available in a wide range of colors which are suitable for use with both pens and brushes.

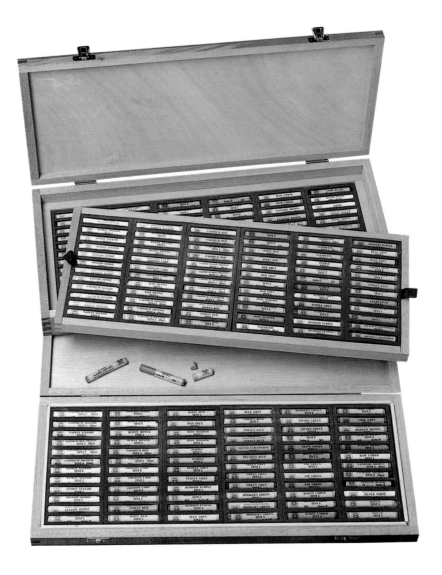

Drawing Equipment and Materials

Brushes

In Chinese art, there is no definition between the disciplines of drawing and painting. This is because all drawing is done with a brush. Drawing with a brush produces a free-flowing, fluid spontaneity. Any type of ink or paint can be used as a drawing medium, or within a mixed-media composition.

Paper

There is a huge range of drawing paper available, both as individual sheets or in a book form such as a drawing pad or sketchbook. Drawing paper is graded according to its weight (gsm, or grams per meter squared), which determines its thickness, and can be bought in a range of sizes and colors. Some paper is textured to produce certain effects or to suit specific materials, whereas other papers are fairly universal and can be used with most drawing mediums.

Often quite unusual effects can be achieved according to the paper type that is used, so it is worth experimenting with lots of different types of paper.

- Smooth paper is good for pencil sketches and pen and ink, as detailed compositions can be created without the drawing medium "bleeding" into the paper. The lines will appear clean and fine. Cartridge paper is an excellent all-round paper for most types of sketching and sketch-books are often made from it. Hot-pressed paper is very smooth and gives a hard, unforgiving line whereas cold-pressed paper is a little more textured so lines appear softer. Felt tip pens are best used with hot-pressed paper or card as they bleed easily.

- Textured paper is essential if you are choosing to work with chalk, charcoal or pastels as these drawing mediums will all benefit from having a rougher surface to "key" into. The powdery nature of these types of drawing medium mean that they require a pitted surface in which the pigment can sit. The different grades of paper texture will produce very different effects. Some are very coarse while others give a softer, richer tone.

- Colored paper adds an extra dimension, especially to pastel and chalk drawings. The most famous colored paper is Ingres paper, which comes in every imaginable shade and has a soft, velvety surface which makes it ideal for delicate work. Cheap sugar paper is also suitable and is a cost-effective sketching paper.

When looking at the "weight" of drawing paper, remember that:

- 150 gsm is a good basic sketching and drawing paper.

- 180 gsm is a heavier paper more suited to charcoal and soft pencil compositions.

- 300 gsm is good for colored pencil washes, watercolor and pen washes, and mixed-media.

Other accessories

- Putty eraser: this is a malleable eraser, which can be used to lift pigment off paper, to remove lines or create highlights. It can actually be shaped by hand into a point to erase very small areas of pigment. Putty erasers tend not to damage paper in the way a harder eraser might.

- Hard eraser: hard erasers are better suited for pencil drawings on smooth paper. They are very effective at removing lines, but take care not to rub too hard as you may damage the paper.

- Paper stump: paper stumps are used to blend pigment together in a more delicate way than a finger could achieve. They are sometimes referred to as torchons and are rolled strips of paper which can be sharpened and reused.

- Drawing board: this is a piece of board onto which you can clip or tape your paper to ensure it does not slip about when you are working.

- Fixative: this is a spray varnish which helps to bind the pigment of materials such as chalk or pastel to the drawing surface to prevent it from slipping or smudging.

- Craft knives and sharpeners: these are essential to keep your pencils in top condition, especially when doing fine, detailed drawings. Craft knives are very useful as they sharpen pencils, cut paper, and can be used as a drawing tool in their own right. Use the tip of a craft knife to scratch into paper to lift away pigment for an unusual effect.

Drawing Equipment and Materials

Creating your kit

It is useful to keep all your art materials together to keep them in good condition and easily accessible when something grabs your imagination. An excellent storage solution is to buy a plastic toolbox from a hardware store, as it will have lots of compartments to keep things in, is light, easy to clean, and has a carrying handle.

Another good investment is an art folder, which is a briefcase-style case with a zipper, which will protect your loose papers and can store your precious compositions.

List of basic drawing equipment

This is a list of the very basics. Add to them as you become more confident in experimenting with different materials.

- 2H, HB, 2B, 4B and 6B pencils

- A putty eraser

- A hard eraser

- A small box of water-soluble colored pencils

- A box of stick charcoal

- A small box of pastels

- Red, blue, and yellow watercolor tubes

- No. 2 and No. 4 watercolor brushes. A larger brush for color washes

- A fine tipped black fiber pen, a black mapping pen, and a black marker pen

- A small bottle of black ink

- A larger, bound sketchbook

- A small spiral-bound sketchpad

- A pad of cartridge paper (150 gsm)

- A pad of cartridge paper (180 gsm)

- A pad of watercolor paper (300 gsm)

- A few sheets of sugar paper in a variety of colors

- A can of fixative

- A craft knife

- Paper tissues for wiping and blending

- Masking tape for securing work onto a drawing board.

You needn't spend a small fortune on putting together the best equipment for achieving your artistic goals

Choosing a Subject

Learn to "See" not "Look"

Most compositions tend to be from direct observation such as still life, portrait or landscape drawing, or painting. As a beginner, you will spend a lot of time observing a wide range of subjects as you plan and create your compositions.

You can find inspiration for your compositions all around you

An artist has to learn to look at the world through new eyes. All those things which you previously took for granted must be viewed afresh, in order for you to break a subject down into its various components: form, tone, texture, color, etc.

- Learn to see rather than simply look. Train your eye to constantly be aware of how things relate to each other to help you plan successful compositions. For example, sit down and look around your room. Begin to break down each item in your eye-line into simple shapes, then observe the way in which those shapes relate to one another—do they overlap? How are they grouped? Where does your eye naturally rest? How could they be made into a pleasing composition? Do the same again, but think about texture, tone, or color.

- Use a subject in two different ways–accurate observation or subjective starting point. Take an object, person or view and, using the exercise above, look at them in a very analytical, objective way, as if you were doing a representational composition. Think about what you see. Then, move away from your subject for a while. When you return, begin imagining how this subject affects you, what it makes you feel. How would you begin to think about representing this subject in a more emotive, subjective way?

- Don't assume that a subject is always the same. Remember that objects, spaces, and subjects can alter according to factors such as time, light, mood, etc.

- Will the subject dictate the medium and/or style of the drawing or painting? Think about the practicalities–if you are quickly sketching skies, or a busy market, then pencil, pens or watercolors will capture the essence of the subject and are portable. A still life could be tackled in pastels or oils with plenty of time for fixing or drying.

What is your objective? Think about what the composition is–a sketch? Research material? A finished composition? Is it objective or subjective? Think about the previous exercises and how you can relate them to your aims for a particular picture. Try to communicate your perception of the subject. Don't be afraid to ask questions, and be enquiring about how the materials you are using will affect technique, structure, and form.

- Keep attempting different subjects. The more you draw and the wider your subject knowledge and understanding, the quicker you will begin to develop your own style and imaginative confidence.

- You can invent your compositions–but you need to have basic technical knowledge and foundation skills to turn imagination into art. Connecting the visual to the technical will allow you greater artistic freedom.

- Develop your hand-to-eye coordination. Remember to allow your own interpretation of the subject to shape your composition and give it warmth and depth.

If you can maintain a certain amount of enthusiasm for the subject, even though you are thinking about the technical aspects of creating a composition, you should be halfway to creating a visually stimulating piece.

There's no need to create a finished materpiece as soon as you sit down— do your research, make visual notes, and plan that imaginative painting

31

To become an artist, and to think and feel the way an artist does, requires patience and practice. A few minutes sketching each day will ensure that your brain, eye and hand coordination improves quickly, allowing you to attempt increasingly challenging techniques and compositions.

Developing your Skills

Many artists spend a lot of time between compositions practicing their techniques, collecting information about subjects which inspire them, collating and developing that information, and experimenting with ideas. The ideal place to gather together all these various elements is within a sketchbook.

- One of the best ways of following your artistic progression is to create a sketchbook which you can practice in every day. Imagine it as an exercise program–15 minutes each day will keep you in trim artistically.

What is a sketchbook?

A sketchbook is an essential piece of equipment which should be used as an artistic aid. In it you will do several things: practice, experiment, keep notes and records, and most importantly, build your confidence.

The practical considerations when purchasing a sketchbook are:

- How big is it? There is no point in having a sketchbook which is too big to transport easily. However, it needs to be big enough to hold the information you require comfortably. A good solution is to have two sketchbooks running concurrently–a small one for keeping in a pocket or handbag at all times, and a larger one for home and location studies.

- What is it made of? It should be hardback or spiral-bound cartridge paper, although if you prefer working in a certain medium, such as pen and ink, pastel or watercolor, you may wish to purchase a sketchbook with paper that is more suitable for that technique. General drawing, sketching, and note-taking will still be required at times, no matter what your choice of medium, so you will need a basic sketchbook as well.

How do I use a sketchbook?

Remember that a sketchbook is not a finished composition. Think of it as a personal visual and technical aid. You can develop your confidence without fear of judgement, as you can make as many mistakes as you wish. Make a point of practicing some sketches without an eraser of any kind–this way you will see the mistakes you have made and can refer to them the next time you go to draw that subject.

- **Practice**–use the sketchbook to try new techniques and hone your skills. Everything from small studies of different lines and textures, rules of perspective or attempting sketches of individual subjects can be tried out within its pages.

- **Experiment**–attempt new things regularly, whether it be a different medium or technique. You can even invent your own ways of mixing mediums together to produce unusual effects. Some may not work, but you will learn a lot from trying.

- **Record keeping**–one of the crucial functions of a good sketchbook is to act as a reference point for more finished compositions. Use it to record detail which will have an influence on the final composition: texture, tone, detail of color, etc.

Look at the subject from different angles and make brief sketches to help you visualize it more clearly when you are finalizing the structure of the picture.

Sketchbook exercises

- Divide a page into four equal boxes. Choose a subject—such as a piece of fruit or a view from your window—and draw it four times over a week. See how your interpretation changes. You should find that the sketches become more fluid.

- Limit yourself to a time, say 30 seconds or two minutes, then sketch something within that time frame. Do this each day for a week and see how much quicker you get at capturing the essence of a subject.

- Collect postcards, cuttings from magazines, interesting scraps of fabric, and photographs. Paste them into your sketchbook for reference and as a starting point for a composition. Visually stimulating items will help fire your imagination.

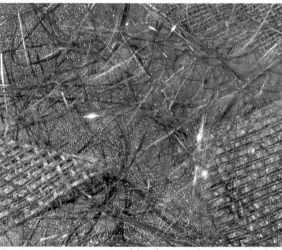

Do two minute exercises like the one shown on the left or a simple one minute portrait sketch like the one of the man in the cap on the top right of the page

- Try limiting yourself to three or four colors. You will learn how to blend more quickly if you have less of a range to choose from.

- Experiment with different ways of making marks in your sketchbook. Use the other end of a pencil or paint brush, or your fingers, dipped in ink or paint to see what marks you can make. An old comb or toothbrush can be dragged through paint or ink to make interesting textures.

- If a subject has lots of exciting qualities, make several sketches which focus on each one in turn: form, detail, color, tone, or texture for example.

- Attempt to create an abstract interpretation from an everyday object.

- These exercises can be repeated over and over again using different subjects, materials, and colors. Try to do at least two a week to keep artistically "fit."

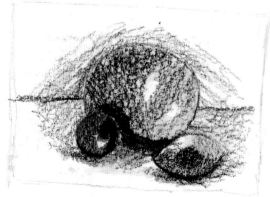

Using a sketchbook on field trips

One of the most important functions of your sketchbook is to be a portable studio. This means that you can easily capture things of interest while you are out and about. Many artists find a great deal of their inspiration occurs when they are outdoors, among nature and everyday scenes. If you have a sketchbook and pencil handy, you will be able to make quick sketches which can be developed into a completed picture at a later date.

Sometimes you will make pre-planned trips, at other times a subject will grab you when you least expect it, so keep that sketchbook to hand at all times.

If you are planning a field trip to study a certain subject, you should make some basic preparations to make your trip as worthwhile as possible.

Planning a sketching trip

It is a good idea to be prepared for a sketching field trip. There are a few basic steps that you can take to make sure you do not have a wasted journey.

• Be prepared for changes in the weather–some places may be fine one minute, then pouring with rain the next. However, this doesn't mean that you cannot collect some valuable material–after all, the weather will give an interesting perspective on the subject. Take a raincoat which can be folded and stored at the bottom of a waterproof rucksack. Also, take some refreshments and dress appropriately, as you will not be inclined to sit sketching if you are too hot or too cold.

• Choose a sturdy bag, such as a rucksack, for

carrying all your materials in as you may want to travel quite far to view certain subjects. A good waterproof bag will last for a long time and will protect your equipment.

• Take a range of sketching materials as you may wish to capture different aspects of a subject which are better suited to certain types of medium. Remember to take a bottle of water along if you intend to use watercolors or water-soluble pencils.

• Take a craft knife to sharpen pencils and create scratching effects. Also pack an eraser, a soft clean rag, and a selection of brushes plus paper clips to stop your papers from blowing about.

• Some people like to have a small, collapsible stool to sit on. A plastic sheet will make a comfortable, easily transportable and light alternative.

When you are working outdoors, you will not be in control of your subject in the way that you are over a still life. You may find that the scene or subject that you are trying to capture is constantly changing, so you will have to learn to sketch quickly.

• Don't waste time on elements of the subject which can be left out or added later on.

• Make a few notes to support your sketch to help you remember details.

• Focus on the essential information that you need to capture, and choose an approach and the materials that will help you to do this.

- If you are not able to sketch your intended subject for some reason, then try something else– you may be pleasantly surprised by the results.

- Remember, your intended subject may not be as helpful as you would like. Animals have a habit of moving around, as do people, so you may find you have to attempt several sketches at the same time. That way, you can return to each one as the animal shifts to and from a particular position.

Supporting material

You may find that you want to take some photographs or notes to help support your sketches, which will aid you when developing them into a final composition. You can make your initial sketches in pencil or charcoal, then use a photograph to provide information about color, or a few written notes explaining the quality of the light.

- Use photographs to give you a range of compositional viewpoints.

- A general reminder of the scene or subject is useful when creating a final picture.

- Capture specific elements, such as color or form, in a photo which can be referred to later.

- Use a photograph as inspiration for starting a composition.

- Certain subjects, such as a bird flying, can be captured on camera more easily than in a sketch, and then used as the basis for a finished piece.

However, do not rely on photographs alone when composing a picture. Copying a photo will result in a dull, lifeless piece of art.

Make location sketch notes to help you remember details about a scene or subject. You can also incorporate these notes into a sketch for additional reference. Simple words or bullet points will enable you to cross-reference several drawings and photographs far more easily.

Field study exercises

- Choose a view that inspires you, and over the course of several visits, sketch it using different mediums and from different viewpoints. When you feel you have really got to know the scene, attempt a composition from memory, drawing on the essence of the subject, as opposed to the technical details.

- When sketching wildlife, limit yourself to a time –say 30 seconds–so you can attempt to create a fluid representation which contains the very basic elements of the subject. Zoos, nature reserves, and parks are great places to study different types of creatures. Concentrate on the overall posture and proportions rather than detail.

- Choose a subject such as a flower or tree, then sketch it over a period of weeks. You will learn how it changes and alters according to the seasons, weather, and light quality. Decaying plants can produce fantastic shapes and textures.

- Choose a theme, such as trees or buildings, and gather together as much information in the form of sketches, photographs, and magazine clippings. Be on the lookout for any interesting examples when you are on your travels.

- Always take your sketchbook with you when you go on vacation. Different countries have a vast array of wildlife, landscapes, buildings, and people that can provide you with new subjects to tackle. Many of these will inspire you as you view them, so be sure to take plenty of notes to allow you to create a composition when you return home.

- Try sketching a scene at different times of the day. The light quality in the early morning will be entirely different to that at dusk. Watch how the shadows fall and the tonal values change.

Try to complete at least one of these activities each week, even if you choose a view from your window. There is nothing like sketching from life to give your compositions a firm foundation of form and structure. Knowing how something moves, grows or changes according to the weather, light, and conditions will enable you as an artist to interpret your chosen subject with far more clarity and feeling.

The following chapters contain exercises that are ideal for practicing in a sketchbook. That way you will have a continuous record of your improvement as an artist.

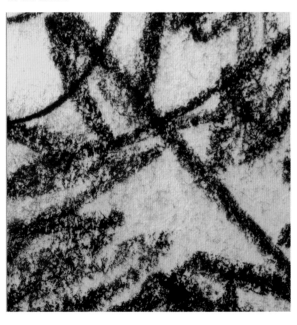

BASIC SHAPE

Deep yellow

Ultramarine

Violet

White

Applying paint

Add detail

Blended

Making Marks

Lines, Texture, and Tone

Follow these simple exercises to begin mastering your pencil work and your experimentation with different types of medium. Remember that practice is very important if you want to start on the road to becoming an accomplished artist.

Exercise 1

Exercise 2

Exercise 3

LESSON 1

One of the most important things you need to learn before you even make a mark is how to hold your drawing equipment. There are essentially two ways of holding a pencil or other drawing implement. Most people will grip the implement, for example a pencil, near the drawing point, then move their fingers and wrist to produce a tight linear control, as you would when writing.

The other way is to hold the pencil more lightly, releasing the tension from the fingers and wrist. The drawing action should instead come from the shoulder and through the elbow, with the wrist acting as a shock absorber and remaining loose and fluid. The shaft of the pencil can be held further up, depending on the type of mark you wish to make– the higher up your fingers, the more fluid and loose the line. Try to avoid resting your hand or wrist on the paper as you draw.

Exercise 1

Take an HB pencil, holding it as if you were about to write your name, and draw the looped, wavy and zigzag lines indicated. You should find that it feels quite restrictive drawing with a tense hand and wrist.

Exercise 2

Now, using the same pencil, move your fingers up the pencil shaft and repeat the exercises. This time you should find that there is more fluidity in your wrist, and that the action should come from your shoulder.

Exercise 3

Repeat the exercises again, this time holding the pencil shaft even further up. Really move your arm as you draw, allowing the pencil to travel lightly and smoothly across the page. The lines should appear very free and spontaneous. Compare the three exercises and see the difference that simply changing the position of your hand can make.

Exercise 4

Now draw the looped circles with the technique from Exercise 2. Each time concentrate on keeping the line evenly spaced, continuous, and fluid.

Exercise 5

Your hand, wrist and arm should be loose now. Using the HB pencil, make the range of marks shown. Don't worry if you feel that you are making mistakes—simply repeat any marks you are not comfortable with until you are happy. The marks should allow you to experiment with wrist movement and moving your pencil in different ways over the paper. Repeat the exercises with a 2B pencil to see the effects that can be produced by using another grade of pencil.

Exercise 4

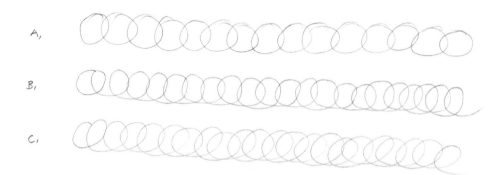

Exercise 5

Exercise 6

Exercise 7

Exercise 6

This grid is made with HB, 2B, and 4B pencils, and combines a wide range of strokes: vertical, horizontal, short, long, angular, and curved. Each box contains a mixture of the pencil grades to show how one type of mark can vary according to the materials or pressure used. This is a useful bank of marks which you can refer to when attempting to create texture in a composition. Copy these or make up some.

Exercise 7

Although it may seem as though there are an indefinite number of lines to be made, in fact there are four basic types. The four boxes are drawn using these lines to show how one object can change according to its linear quality. These lines are:

- **Wire line**–this is a clean, constant line which is used for sharp, definite outlines.

- **Calligraphic line**–a more uneven line as the width is variable, making it useful for emphasizing tonal qualities.

- **Broken line**–this is a short line which is used repeatedly to convey a more subtle outline.

- **Repeated line**–a free-flowing, fluid type of line which has an organic feel. It is a series of loosely parallel lines which build up to form an outline.

Draw these boxes, then attempt a circle or shape to get used to applying the different lines to an object.

Exercise 8

The three techniques shown are examples of methods used by artists to give the feel of three-dimensional tone to an object. Lines are repeatedly criss-crossed either in a regular or random way. This is known as hatching, for lines going in one direction, or cross-hatching for lines which oppose each other. These strokes may be straight or curved.

You should now feel a little more confident about how to use a graphite pencil and the effects that can be created by simply altering the type of stroke, pressure, and hand position. Keep practicing so you become confident in using these basic marks as they will be the foundation of any composition.

LESSON 2

Now you have grasped the basics of handling a pencil, you can begin to experiment with other types of medium. The following exercises will help you to use a wide range of materials to make interesting marks.

Exercise 1

Use a 6B pencil to make a range of marks. See if you can think up a few of your own. Don't be afraid to experiment–smudge with your fingers, press very hard or as lightly as you can, use the tip or the edge of the pencil, and vary your hand movements.

Exercise 2

Do exactly the same as before, but this time use colored pencils. Try cross-hatching two or more different colors to see what effects you can achieve.

Exercise 3

These marks are made with wax crayons. Using a craft knife, scratch into the cross-hatching to create interesting marks and effects.

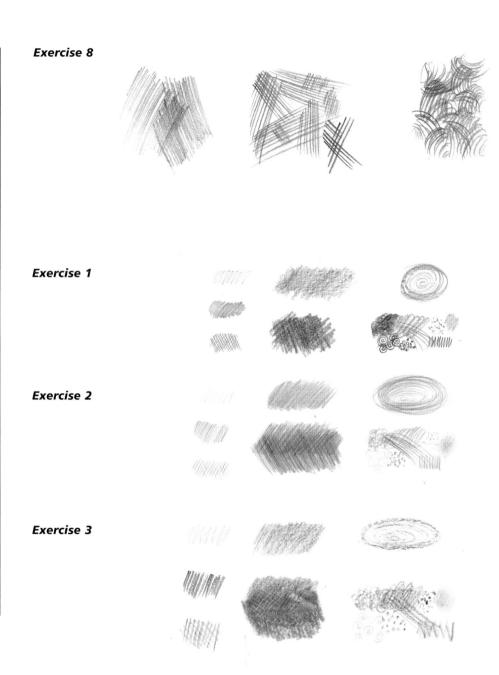

Exercise 8

Exercise 1

Exercise 2

Exercise 3

Making Marks

Exercise 4—5

Exercise 4

Use a charcoal stick to make bold expressive marks which feel quite different to pencil. Get messy—work the charcoal with your fingers to make tonal forms.

Exercise 5

Do the same as you did with the charcoal stick, but this time, use a charcoal pencil to understand the subtle differences between the two similar materials.

Exercise 6

Use some scraps of colored sugar or Ingres paper to see how certain materials react to a colored background. The materials shown here are, from left to right: a pastel stick, a white chalk pencil, sanguine oil pencil, carbon stick, sepia light pencil. Experiment using other mediums to see the range of effects you can produce.

Exercise 7

This example shows how colored backgrounds affect materials. A range of oil pastels are used to highlight the difference between light and dark backgrounds and how they change the way we see the color of the applied medium.

Exercise 8

Oil pastels can be overlaid, hatched, scratched, smudged, and applied with degrees of pressure to produce a range of effects and color combinations. This exercise would also work well with chalk and soft pastels.

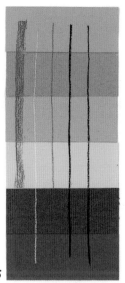

Exercise 6

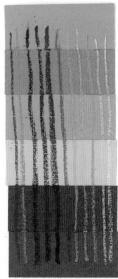

Exercise 7

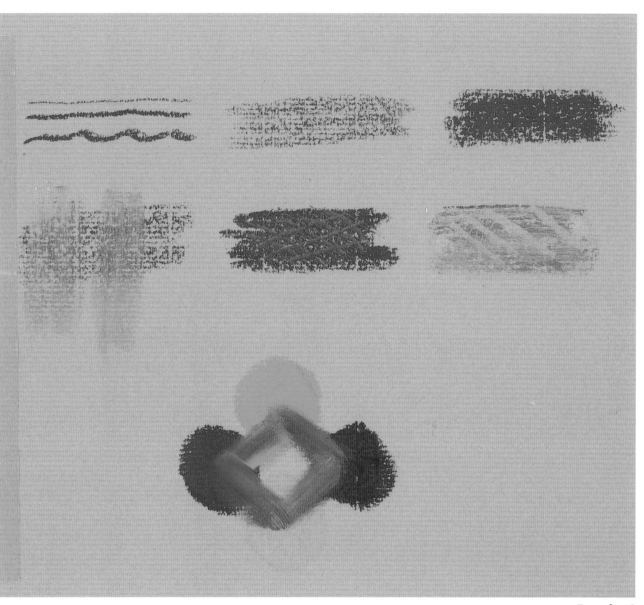

Exercise 8

Making Marks

Exercise 9

Exercise 9
Use a range of pens–ballpoint, mapping pens, calligraphy nibs and felt tips or markers–to make a range of marks. See how some pens can give a varied line, while others are more consistent.

Extra exercise
Make your own mark boards, like the two shown. Be very free and expressive. See how the different lines and marks interact with each other.

46

LESSON 3

You now have the basic techniques to enable you to begin to create pictures. You will be able to use the marks as the building blocks for producing texture and tone within your compositions.

Tone is a measure of light and dark within a painting or drawing and refers to the amount of light which reaches your eyes when you look at a color. A black and white photograph is made up of tones captured by the camera, so we are able to recognize the images within the photograph even though we do not know what color they are. When you are applying tone to a composition, think of the subject as if it were a black and white photograph to help you recognize where the dark, mid and light areas of tone are situated.

Exercise 1

Make a tone scale board. Draw nine squares, then color the last square black. Now work backwards through to the last square, decreasing the tone as you go. The final square should be almost white. The paper you draw on will represent absolute whiteness.

Exercise 2

Using three of the tones from the tone board, copy the simple landscape. Concentrate on maintaining the three tones consistently throughout the composition.

Exercise 2

Exercise 1

Exercise 3

Exercise 3

Now try using four tones. Copy the simple scene, and then try applying a different range of tones to it. Think about how the light will affect tone–imagine a sunny day and how a dark shadow can affect the tonal quality of a subject.

Exercise 4

Have a go at a very simple tonal still life, like the flowers in a vase shown. Don't worry about too much detail. Instead, think about how to break the picture down into shades of dark and light. Use cross-hatching techniques to give shape and form to your drawing. You can give a feeling of perspective

Exercise 4

by using areas of light and shade to shape objects, giving them a three-dimensional quality.

You should now feel more confident about how to recognize areas of tone and how to apply them in a composition.

Extra exercise
Try the above exercises, this time using color–pencils, pastels, etc. Remember to restrict the number of colors, and use the darker colors to represent the heavier areas of tone.

The pastel drawing of the South Downs, England on a windy morning is a colored tonal composition using only five colors to capture the qualities of the mood and light.

Making Marks

LESSON 4

It is now possible to pull all the previous exercises together to start making interesting compositions using a range of marks to indicate line, tone, and texture.

Look at the drawing of the frog. It is a pen drawing which looks incredibly complicated but is actually made up of three marks–dots, circles, and straight lines–which give the composition depth and texture.

Exercise 1

Take an ordinary household object, such as the cup shown. Draw its basic shape, then use simple hatching techniques to add tone and depth. Now try to draw the same object using dots.

Exercise 2

Continue the theme from Exercise 1, this time adding more detail, texture, and tone to your drawing. Experiment with lots of different types of lines and marks to see how a subject can be interpreted in different ways, according to the method of line you use, such as the three bottles.

Exercise 3

Begin sketching as many different types of texture that you can find. Look at the way texture has been used in the drawing of the squirrel to give the effect of fur and bark. The pen sketch of the fox is much freer, yet is full of vibrant lines. The ballpoint flower sketch relies on texture to give it interest, as the medium is very constant and can appear boring and lifeless. The frog sketch mixes color and texture

Exercise 1

Exercise 2

to great technical effect, directly contrasting the softer, more fluid feel of the olive tree pencil sketch. Now attempt your own sketches. Look at bricks, trees, plants, animals, fabrics, and anything else around you that is textured. Use your line bank from Lesson 1, Exercise 6, as a guide to the types of mark you can make.

Keep practicing these exercises until you feel really comfortable. You will then be ready to move on to composing beautiful pictures.

The perfect composition, the best textures, the right medium —all can be made redundant without the right use of color. Study this useful guide to making the very most of your palette.

The Basics of Color

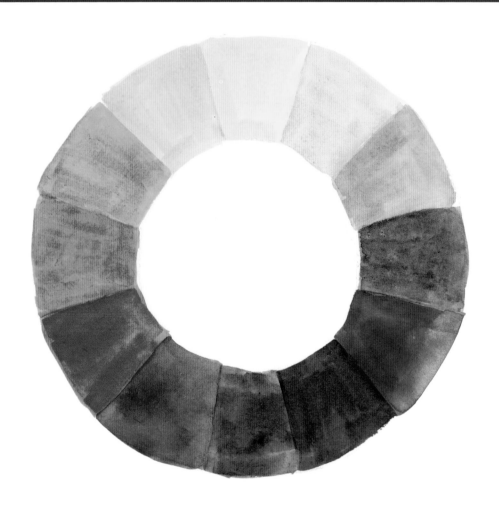

The color wheel

A color wheel will help you to see how the different colors relate to each other, which will assist you when you are mixing colors and applying them to your compositions. The color wheel is a visual representation of the three main qualities that makes up any color. These are hue, tonal value, and intensity.

- A hue is simply the name of a color: red, orange, violet, and burnt sienna are all common examples.

- Tonal value is the darkness or lightness of a color. A hue can be made darker or shaded by adding black pigment, or lighter or tinted by adding white pigment.

- Intensity refers to how bright or dull a hue is. The stronger the intensity, the more brilliant and vivid the color. Yellow is a prime example of a strong intensity, whereas violet is weaker, so appears dull.

- This color wheel is made up of three types of hue: primary, secondary, and tertiary.

Make your own color wheel and keep it in your sketchbook to help you to understand more about using color. Draw a circle and divide it into six equal segments.

Primary colors

A primary color cannot be mixed from any other color. There are three primary colors–red, yellow, and blue. These colors are very pure and bright, and are very easily recognized. Babies are able to see the difference between primary colors early in their development, whereas other, more subtle hues are difficult to distinguish. Paint the three primary colors onto your color wheel, positioning yellow at the top, as indicated.

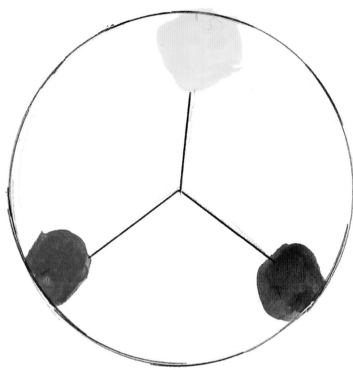

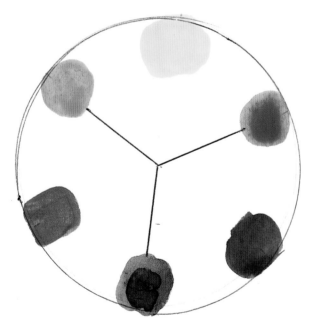

Secondary colors

If you mix yellow and red together, you make orange, which is known as a secondary color. A secondary color is always made using two primary colors. Add yellow to blue, making green, then finally mix blue with red to make violet. Add these to your color wheel as indicated.

53

Complementary colors

Red and green are complementary colors. They are directly opposite on the color wheel and are visually opposed to each other. All primary colors are complemented by a secondary color, never another primary. Use the color wheel to learn which colors complement each other. Complementary colors will stand out within a composition, so should be used sparingly so they do not appear too jarring to the eye.

Colors mixed with black

The colors below from the color wheel have been mixed with black, making the colors shaded. They are duller and darker in appearance.

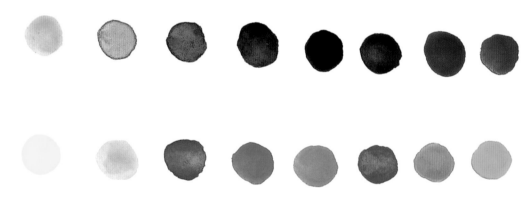

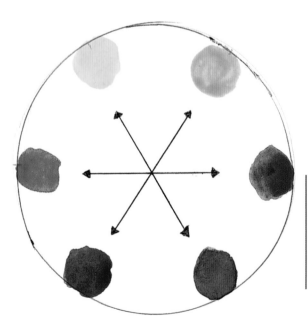

Tertiary colors

Tertiary colors are made by mixing a primary color with a secondary color. Red-orange, yellow-green, and blue-violet are all examples of tertiary colors. Position the tertiary colors on the color wheel between each related primary and secondary color combination.

Colors mixed with white

The above colors from the color wheel have been mixed with white, making the colors tinted. They are softer and lighter in appearance.

Color and mood

Color is able to convey mood within a composition by initiating an emotive response from the viewer. Look at the two photographs. Both are of a similar subject–still water. Yet the mood in each is quite different because of the color.

The photograph of the boat is a tonal value composition, with blue as the predominant color. It is cool, calm, almost unnerving in its quietness. The colors within give a feeling of emptiness, reflected beautifully in the empty boat which appears abandoned.

The other photograph is of a sunset, edging into the night. Although the scene is one of solitude, it still appears warm and inviting as the golden yellow tones radiate across the sky and are reflected in the still water.

This shows how important it is to choose the correct colors when creating a composition. Think about the mood you wish to convey, then use the color wheel to help you select appropriate colors.

Using your Palette

Warm and cool colors can change the mood of a painting dramatically—the pears show perfectly how a subject can change depending on the use of color

Warm/cool colors

If you draw an imaginary line through the color wheel, down from the yellow to the violet, you can split the two halves into warm and cool colors.

The reds and oranges are known as warm–think of the sun, fire, a sunset–whereas the greens and blues are cool–flowing water and lush foliage.

It is normal to use a mixture of both warm and cool colors within a composition, although some striking effects can be created by using just a warm or cool palette. The abstract drawings were each made from oil pastel colors from one side of the color wheel. The pears are also drawn using purely warm or cool colors, to show how a subject can be interpreted in very different ways depending on the colors chosen.

To balance a composition, a mixture of the two palettes should be used. The photographs of the bowl of apples shows how purely tonal colors can make a composition seem cold or lifeless. The predominantly violet and green bowls seem too stark, whereas the yellow bowl is warm and lifelike in appearance.

This is especially true when showing highlights or shadows. If, for example, you are drawing a tree, you can add yellow highlights and blue shadows to show structure and form. Also, you can convey a feeling of depth by adding warm colors to the foreground, while restricting the background to cooler tones.

Light/dark colors

A drawing can be viewed as light or dark, according to the tonal values of the colors used, just as it could be perceived as warm or cool.

Most drawings contain definite areas of light and dark. Each of these can be rich, warm and forward, or cool and recessive. Adding white or black will respectively lighten or darken a color, but these tend to have a cooling effect on the color they are mixed with.

Remember, most white within a composition will be tinted by another hue.

Another way is to add a color which is close to the color you wish to lighten or darken, which will change the hue without cooling it down.

The two pencil landscapes are both drawn with a similar range of colors, although the darker composition contains a far higher ratio of darker hues and tones. It is sombre and oppressive, and the use of the dark paper helps to emphasize this mood. In contrast, the coastal landscape contains much less dark pigment and feels open, bright, and welcoming.

It's the best way to make the move from sketching to progressing your technique—creating a composition based round a still life will increase your confidence while honing your emerging skillset as an artist.

Organizing a Still Life

When you first begin tackling a more complicated composition, as opposed to simple sketches, it is a good idea to begin with a still life.

You may take your time over a still life as you can set it up somewhere without the concern that it will move or change dramatically. This gives you more control over your working conditions.

Do not attempt anything too complicated at first. Instead, set up a simple still life containing two or three basic shapes and colors.

You may position your still life near a natural light source, such as a window, but bear in mind that this will be subject to change. A good alternative is to use an angle-poise lamp which can be directed at the subject to achieve the exact amount of light and shadow you require.

You will also need to decide whether your composition will be landscape or portrait. Normally, the shape of the subject matter will dictate this–a tall vase of flowers is best done as portrait, whereas a scattered fruit bowl is best captured as landscape.

Decide the approach you wish to take. Is it a subjective composition, such as the colorful oil pastel fruit bowl, which is capturing the essence of the subject? Or a more objective viewpoint that will produce a representational picture, such as the watercolor and pen sketch of the flower vase.

Try to make your composition exciting. Look at the groups of objects. The circles work best when there is a variation in size. The bottle, circle, and box form a more interesting composition when they are not arranged in a straight line and the final example shows how objects should be grouped rather than spread out evenly. Try to use a variety of forms, heights, and sizes to give extra interest.

Drawing rounded shapes

You will discover that many of the objects that you choose to create a still life from will contain circles or curves. It is possible to learn to break down any rounded object into three simple shapes–cylinder, cone, and sphere–then add the detail once you have got the basic form down.

If you look at the top of a glass, plate or bottle from straight on, it will appear flat. When you tilt it slightly toward you, you can then see it is rounded. This flattened circular shape is called an ellipse.

- Practice making simple ellipses by lightly holding your pencil and drawing a flattened circle. Repeat this motion, gradually flattening the circle a little more each time, until you feel confident.

- Drawing a simple circle can seem daunting. Keep your wrist relaxed and draw from your shoulder. You will get better the more you practice.

- Don't press too hard as it makes any mistakes more difficult to erase.

Now attempt the three main shapes: cylinder, cone, and sphere.

- To make the shapes appear three-dimensional, practice varying the depth of the ellipse. You will soon realize when you are over or under-drawing the depth as it will make the shape appear distorted.

- Notice how the glass and bottle are made up from a series of ellipses along a central axis line, in the form of cylinders. Look at some common household objects and break them down into the three separate shapes.

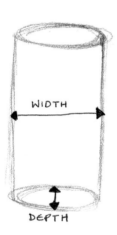

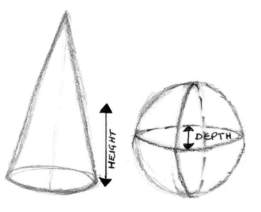

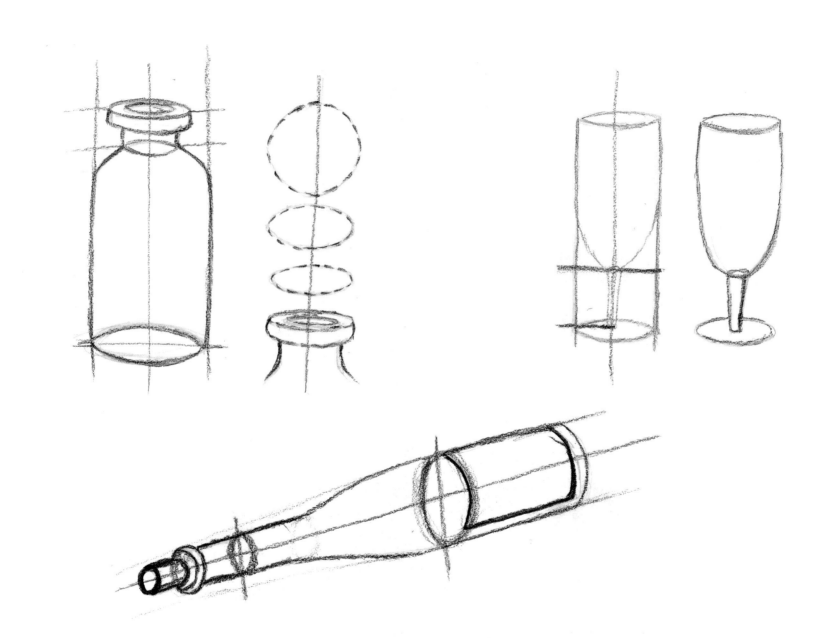

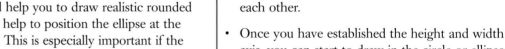

Axis lines

Axis lines will help you to draw realistic rounded objects. They help to position the ellipse at the correct angle. This is especially important if the subject is tilted or at an angle.

• The upright line is the height axis. The horizontal line indicates the depth axis. These lines should always be at right angles to each other.

• Once you have established the height and width axis, you can start to draw in the circle or ellipse. Remember, each quarter mirrors the next.

• Use the horizontal axis to join up two or more ellipses, such as in a bowl or glass. Even if an object is at an angle, the ellipses must still be parallel to one another or the object will appear distorted.

• Try the shapes shown, then attempt to draw some of your own.

Point of view

These six sketches show how important the compositional element of setting up a still life is. The same group of objects can appear completely different when viewed from different angles.

• The first view is looking down, showing the "bird's-eye" view.

• The second view is looking upwards from a "worm's-eye" perspective.

• The third view is straight on at eye level, with no ellipses showing.

• The fourth view is from the side, with the bowl partly obscuring the lower box.

• The fifth view shows the scene from a more conventional front aspect, looking down into the composition.

• The final viewpoint is from behind, with the two large objects obscuring everything else.

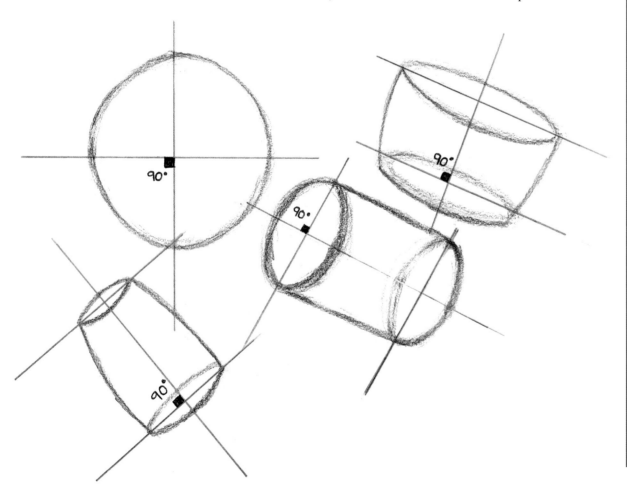

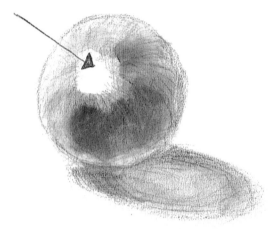

Shadow and light

One of the most important elements of a still life is the lighting and the effects that it creates among the chosen objects. The following examples show how dramatic contrasts can be made by placing the light source in front of the composition, which makes extreme contrasts between light and shadow.

Positioning the light source above the composition creates a quite different effect, which is far more tonal and gives a feeling of solidity. This is a better way of lighting a group of objects as you can see more of the inter-relationship between the various shapes, especially through the intensity of shadow.

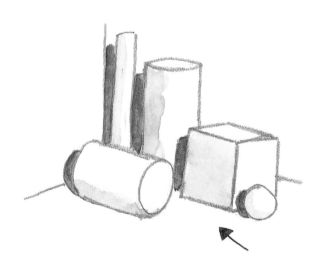

Simple shapes

If you look at any still life, you will notice that the composition can be broken down into simple shapes. Continuing on from the sphere, cone, and cylinder, you can now begin to break down more complicated three-dimensional objects.

- Learn to break objects down into simple shapes. They will be much easier to draw. Add detail once you have captured the basic shape.

- Press lightly when sketching in shapes so any guidelines can easily be erased.

- Remember to always draw a central axis, then arrange the ellipses along it. This applies even if the object is at an angle.

- An ellipse at eye level is shallower than one positioned above or below eye level.

- Just because you cannot see part of an object doesn't mean it is not there. Bear this in mind when you position objects close together in a composition. This will ensure the depth of the composition is not distorted.

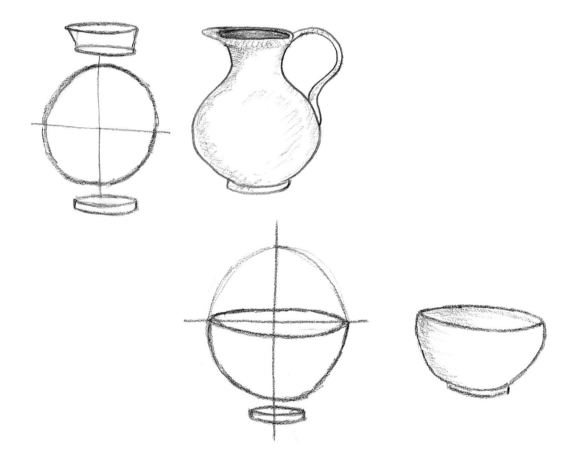

Still life example 1
This simple still life drawing is quite traditional, comprising of a wine bottle with fruit. The composition is very simple and can be broken into simple shapes. It is sketched in pencil, then colored in with water-soluble colored pencils.

- **Step one**–the basic shape is sketched out in pencil, leaving the very pale areas white. The darker, shadowed areas are lightly picked out with slight shading.

- **Step two**–basic areas of color begin to be added, and the guidelines are lightened or erased.

- **Step three**–more color is added and blended directly on the page, using cross-hatching, smudging, and varying the pressure of the applied color to create a translucent effect.

- **Step four**–the final details are added, including highlights in the shiny-skinned fruit and the reflective surface of the glass bottle.

Still life example 2

Many people think that all still life has to be about flowers and fruit. This composition proves that an exciting painting can be produced from a wide variety of subject matter. In this case, the subject is a dog skull.

The composition is very fluid and relaxed, as opposed to formal or stuffy. The brush strokes are vibrant, and while the subject is observational, the use of texture and light is more subjective. The drawing is focusing on the skull, giving a sketchy feel to the surrounding objects.

Remember, some of the best compositions are successful because they are not over-worked. Do not feel that you have to capture every detail. Instead, learn to give the composition space, and focus on the necessary elements which convey meaning and emotion.

- **Step one**–the objects within the still life are broken down into basic, simple shapes with a 2B pencil. The lines can be erased as the finer, more detailed sketch is completed. Keeping the shapes very simple to begin with means that the positional aspects can be changed without having to erase detailed drawings.

- **Step two**–next, basic tonal elements of light and shade are added with a 4B pencil. The shadows are smudged to give a smooth appearance, echoing the texture of the skull.

- **Step three**–finally, more detail is added to the drawing, including a few darker areas picked out with a 6B pencil to add depth and definition. Much of the outer area is left unworked which allows the skull to remain the main focus of the picture. Highlights are created by lifting away pigment using a putty eraser.

It is important to approach a landscape with a certain amount of organization. Although creativity is important, there are several structural elements that should be considered before getting down to the composition.

Organizing a Landscape

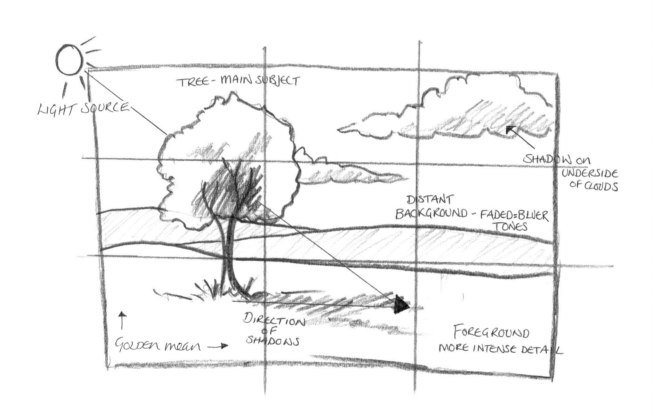

LIGHT SOURCE

TREE - MAIN SUBJECT

SHADOW ON UNDERSIDE OF CLOUDS

DISTANT BACKGROUND - FADED=BLUER TONES

↑ GOLDEN mean →

DIRECTION OF SHADOWS

FOREGROUND MORE INTENSE DETAIL

This is especially true if you are on location, as you will have to factor in environmental influences such as weather and light.

- Make a note of where your light source is. In most cases, this will be the sun, or possibly moonlight or a streetlight if you are working at night. In the field sketch of the tree and hills, you can see the position of the sun, and from that work out where the highlights and shadows will form. Should the light change, you will have a basic reference point.

- Use the Golden Mean principle to divide your composition up. This will ensure that the main subject–in this case the tree–is not positioned too centrally which will detract from the rest of the picture.

- Make a few notes in your sketchbook to help you remember important details that you may need, to ensure consistency throughout the composition.

However, don't be afraid to experiment as sometimes the more a composition breaks the rules, the more effective it is.

Don't forget to do your homework before embarking on a difficult piece

Dark green

church – Sandstone

Pale yellow/green

Purple-grey

Village

River

Wooden fencing

grass

Sandy Banks

Water greeny brown

73

Skies and backgrounds

Skies and background details are crucial elements in any landscape composition–in fact, many artists base their work around particular subjects such as water, sunsets or mountains.

The sunset uses colored pencils to create a dramatic skyscape filled with rich color.

In contrast, the watercolor pencil sketch of a boat is delicate, yet fluid. Everything is simple and representational, yet very effective.

The dramatic, almost abstract mountain scene was created by smudging chalk pastels to suggest the idea of blustery wind.

- Have a go at creating a variety of skies and water effects. Try to be spontaneous–often the best effects are those which you least expect. A natural looking sky or water scene should not be overworked. Use the following examples to help you.

Skyscapes

- Use wet-in-wet washes of ink or watercolor pencil to create a cloudy effect.

- Apply small touches of color to a predominantly white sky to pick out gaps within the clouds.

- Charcoal can be scumbled and smudged to create a tumultuous stormy sky.

Water effects

- Reflections can be picked out using dashes, leaving the white paper to act as the reflected light on the tips of the waves.

- Pencils, pastels or charcoal can be scumbled, dragged, and splattered to create waves and spray.

75

Trees and flowers

Most landscapes will contain some foliage; even industrial areas contain plant life.

Texture is vital when drawing trees and flowers, as it helps to convey the movement of the leaves, the rough bark or delicate flowerheads.

The photograph of the trees shows the dramatic architectural shapes formed by the skeletal branches.

The leaf shapes are not particularly observational, yet possess a quality of natural light and movement.

The sketches of the violets show how much detail can be achieved using simple pencil marks, then enhanced further by adding color.

The blackberry twig is a fluid pen sketch, which is a useful reference. The colored pencil tree is an excellent example of a detailed sketchbook observation.

• Use your sketchbook to collect and practice lots of different types of plant life. Make simple observational sketches that will act as reference material for the future.

The key to drawing trees and flowers successfully is texture

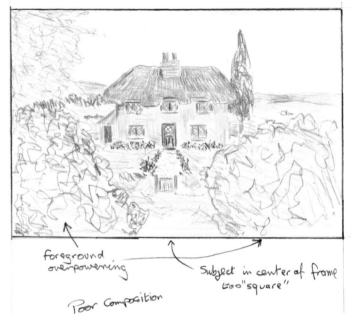

foreground
overpowering

Subject in center of frame
too "square"

Poor Composition

Buildings

Buildings can be quite daunting things for the beginner to tackle, as they are technically more complicated than a more natural subject. The trick is to include the important aspects, leaving out any unnecessary elements, which give a sense of the building without getting overtaken by technicalities. The following examples are different interpretations of how to convey the linear qualities of different types of building, while remaining fluid and interesting.

- The two thatched cottage compositions show the need for careful consideration of where to place the central subject within the wider framework.

- The sketch of a street in Prague conveys the sense of perspective well as your eye travels up the street. There is little detail, but the buildings seem to bustle with interesting architectural elements.

- The drawing of the church gives an even greater indication of the importance of perspective. It reaches upwards, which highlights its significance as an emotionally powerful structure.

- Finally, other elements that require a very linear approach can also be interpreted in interesting and vivacious ways, such as the sketch of a fence post.

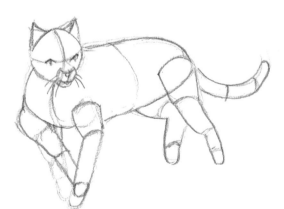

Animals

Many people choose animal sketching as main subjects for their art, as there are so many incredible creatures out there. Animals can be hard to capture, either because they move about too much, or due to the complicated anatomical elements. You can break animals into shapes, as shown in the sketches of the dog, cat, and horse.

Use still images to practice proportions, but always try to see your subject in its natural environment where possible, as this will give you a far greater indication of how it moves and behaves.

Quick sketches may not be as anatomically correct, but will capture the spirit of the subject more comprehensively.

- The linear cat jumping has little detail, yet captures the movement of the leap.

- The sketch of the terrier conveys the charming nature of the subject.

- The sketch of a horse concentrates on the subject's expressive fluidity of movement.

- The tiger sketch concentrates on observing the texture and markings for a future composition.

Make simple sketches in your sketchbook to act as reference material. Always try to convey the essence and spirit of the creature.

Landscape example 1

This simple colored pencil seascape relies on cross-hatching the colors to blend them together. It is a very basic composition, with the emphasis on color to convey a feeling of space and warmth. A basic palette of colors is used: dark and light blue, green, red, yellow, orange, purple, and white.

- **Step one**—sketch out the very basic lines and block in the first colors of the sky, sea, and sand.

- **Step two**—now use a cross-hatching technique to overlap colors to build up the intensity within the composition. Work each layer in the opposite direction from the previous one to allow a certain amount of color to show through. Add the detail of the boat and grasses.

- **Step three**—use a white pencil to soften the entire composition by cross-hatching over the color layers. Pick out shadows and highlights on the boat and grasses, using complementary colors.

Landscape example 2

This landscape is drawn with charcoal, and highlights are added with chalk. It is a simple, stylized composition that is subjective in nature. Everything is exaggerated, from the foliage of the trees, through the depth of shadows, up to the brooding storm clouds.

- **Step one**—sketch in the basic outline of the drawing. Block in the darkest areas and draw in the tree trunks and branches.

- **Step two**—begin to add more tonal areas, with the foreground containing the strongest tones which fade towards the background to give a feeling of depth. Add the foliage to the trees in a circular motion and smudge to soften the lines. Repeat this technique to build up the storm clouds.

- **Step three**—finally, pick out more detail with the tip of the charcoal. Add light tones to the tree and clouds by smudging in a little white chalk.

Landscape example 3

This sketch was done on location using a mapping pen. It concentrates on capturing the mood and feel of the subject. The mountains were quite brooding and foreboding, but they were softened by the softer, more textural qualities of the various grasses and foliage.

- **Step one**–a few preliminary sketches were made to decide what types of mark were most appropriate to convey the wide array of textures within the composition.

- **Step two**–a basic linear sketch was put down, keeping the pen lines fluid and light as any mistakes could not be removed. The darker areas of tone were sketched in.

- **Step three**–the foreground detail was added, with emphasis on maintaining a feeling of space and natural grandeur, without relying too heavily on individual, highly detailed areas.

Landscape example 4

This townscape is an interesting composition as it relies on the mix of rough pencil and mapping pen lines to convey a feeling of energy and movement to capture the hustle and bustle of a busy street.

- **Step one**–sketch in the linear sketch with an HB pencil. The lines are representational as opposed to observational. You should be sketching in very basic shapes to represent figures and objects.

- **Step two**–now begin to add more detail and tone with a 4B pencil. Again, ensure that you keep all your lines very fluid and sketchy. If you make a mistake, don't worry as it will not detract from the overall composition.

- **Step three**–finally, use a medium-nibbed pen to sketch in details and the main outlines to lift the composition. Keep your wrist very relaxed and draw quickly and smoothly to maintain a feeling of movement and energy.

Proportions of Figures

The human figure is one of the most commonly featured subjects in art throughout history, as it is constantly changing according to the pose or gesture of the subject. It is also notoriously difficult to accomplish.

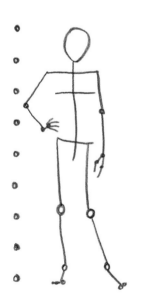
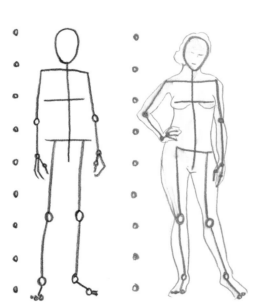

There are some guidelines that make it a little easier to attempt to create a realistic, proportionately accurate figure. Look at the matchstick figures of the man and woman, then at the fully-drawn figures. These figures have been drawn using a method which dates back to the Renaissance period, and which is still the most commonly used method of judging proportion today.

- Although no two figures are the same, it is helpful to have a basic guide from which you can judge the correct proportion.

- The most common method was first used by Renaissance artists.

- To judge a figure's proportion, use the head as a unit of measurement. The average male is usually about eight heads tall.

- The distance from the chin to the crotch— the torso—is normally three heads tall. The torso can be divided into equal thirds at the navel and nipples.

- The distance from the upper leg to the knee is two heads tall, as is the lower leg.

- The distance between the shoulders is roughly two heads wide.

- The elbows are roughly three heads length from the top of the head.

- The wrists should be roughly parallel with the crotch, although this will change according to the stance of the figure.

The female figure is slightly smaller than the male, and has two wide points—the shoulders and hips—both of which measure around two heads width.

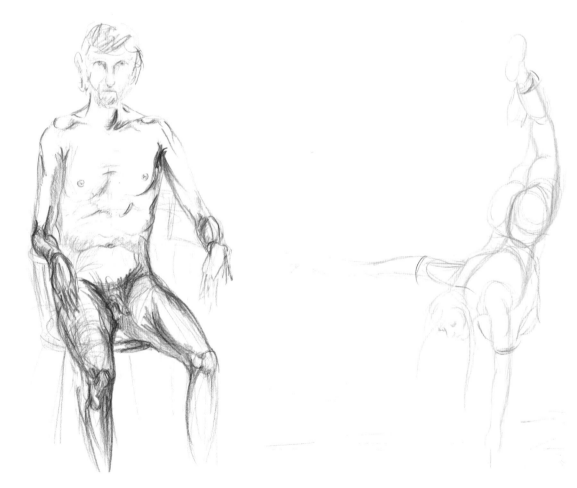

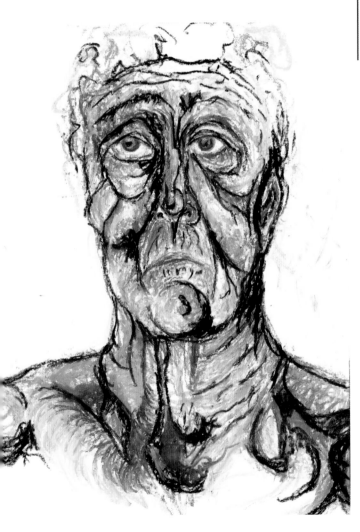

Proportions of the head

Drawing the human head is one of the hardest things for an artist to master, and it will take years of practice to become truly competent. However, there is no reason why you should not begin to think about how to structure a portrait.

It is easier to think of the head as an egg on a cylinder. This egg can then be divided up into rough proportions, which give a basic, stylized version of a human head and features. It is crucial to remember that every face is different, so you will have to develop the ability to turn generic proportions into something that is lifelike and vibrant through practice and experimentation.

- Look at the two structured heads. They are divided up proportionally by the rule of halves. In your sketchbook, draw an egg shape like the ones shown.

- Divide the egg horizontally in half. This marks where the eyes should be positioned.

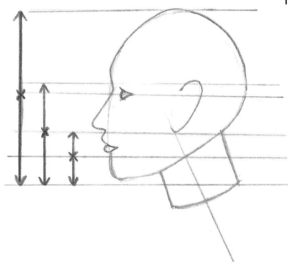

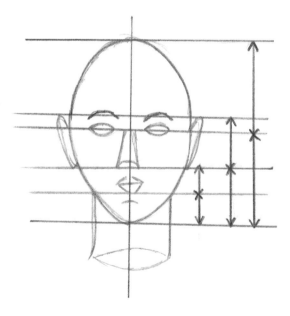

- Position a second line slightly above the eye line to mark where the eyebrows would go.

- Using this eyebrow line, divide the area below in half horizontally. This halfway point is where the base of the nose would be positioned.

- Divide the area below the nose line in half to give the position of the lower lip.

- You should now be able to sketch in the basic features of the human head in their correct positions.

This face is neither male nor female, young nor old. Normally, a woman's features are softer and less defined than a man's. In older people, the features become more pronounced, whereas children tend to have small noses and mouths but comparably large eyes.

There's no need to be literal when drawing a portrait as the compositions here show—it's more important to capture the character of the subject

89

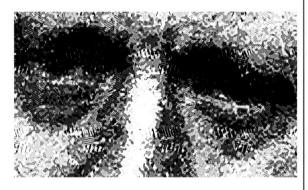

Portrait detail

The best way to become more confident when drawing figures is to make lots of quick sketches of different parts of the body doing different things. Always try and draw from real life, whether you get someone to pose for you, or just sit in a crowded place and make quick sketches of the people who pass you.

Also remember that the human body is affected by the way the person sits or stands, so you may find that the rules of proportion alter slightly. This is particularly true when you draw a figure close up as, just as with a still life or landscape, the human body is affected by the laws of perspective. This means that the parts of the figure closest to you will seem proportionally larger.

To begin with, keep to sketching figures and portraits from the front, back or side, to get you used to the technique without having to deal with anything overcomplicated.

Above all, keep practicing as much as possible. Before long, you will feel ready to attempt more complex poses.

The step-by-step examples on these pages will help you to attempt the harder aspects of portrait and figure drawing, such as eyes, noses, mouths, hands, and feet. Always break the subject up into simple shapes, then add the detail once you are happy with the proportion and positioning.

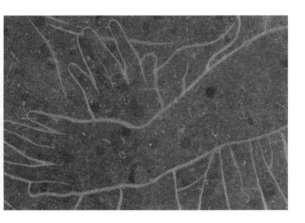

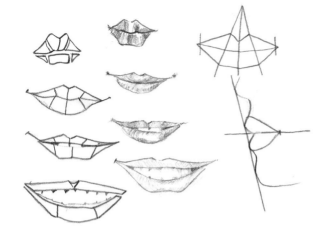

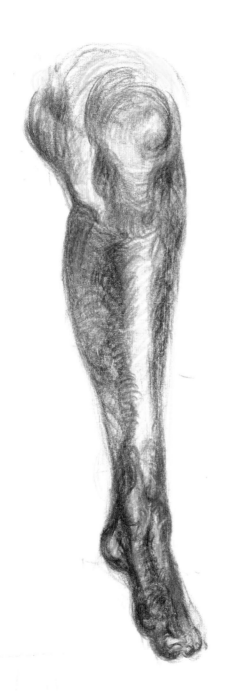

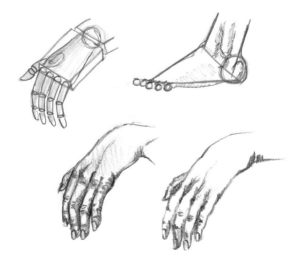

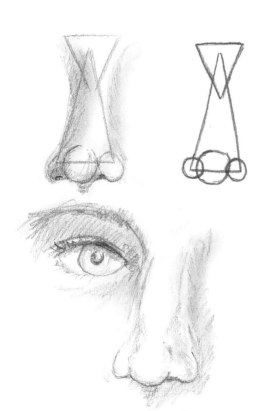

Portrait example 1

These three simple drawings show how you can convey movement by manipulating a simple framework, then "flesh out" the figure around it.

- **Step one**–remembering the rules of proportion, sketch out a framework to help you manipulate a basic figure into interesting poses.

- **Step two**–next, sketch the outline of the figures around the framework.

- **Step three**–finally, add the details that will give your figures a feeling of character and purpose.

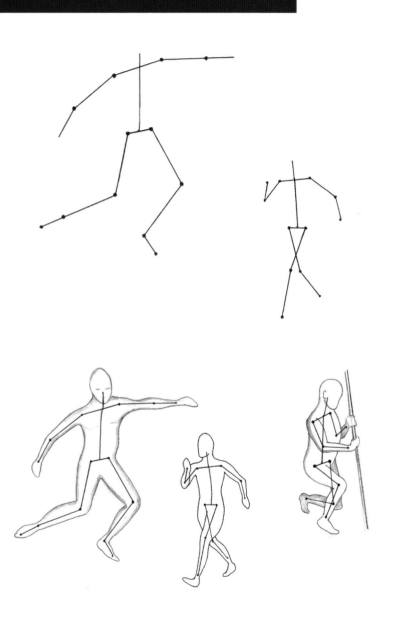

Portrait example 2

This simple charcoal drawing is of an Indian girl. It shows that charcoal can be used to produce a delicate tonal study, which is expressive and observational.

- **Step one**–first, sketch out the face using the rules of proportion, keeping the lines light so mistakes can easily be rectified.

- **Step two**–begin to add in the main areas of shadow, and smudge to soften the lines so as to give a skin-like appearance. Darken the eyes, nostrils and lips.

- **Step three**–lift out pigment to highlight areas using a putty eraser. Define the hair and features with the tip of the charcoal stick and darken the deepest shadows.

Portrait example 3

This drawing is done with oil pastels, and is a step forward from the framework figures. It is of a dancing nude, and is more subjective and stylized, allowing the expressive nature of the movement to become the focal point of the picture.

- **Step one**–sketch out the basic figure, using yellow ochre, medium yellow, and violet.

- **Step two**–begin to build up tonal areas of light and dark color, gently smudging the edges to blend the areas of color together. Use flesh tones, yellows, and cobalt blue to add definition to the figure.

- **Step three**–warm the composition up with a few lowlights of rich brown, and smudge in a little white as highlights.

Portrait example 4

This is a more traditional formal portrait of a young woman, drawn with colored pencils and graphite stick.

Step one–draw in the main contours of the face and define the features with the graphite stick. Add a little detail, such as eyebrows, lip tone, and hair texture.

- **Step two**–begin to add color by lightly cross-hatching the face, overlapping colors to blend new tones. Keep the strokes very light, adding more layers to increase the intensity. This will give the skin a youthful bloom.

- **Step three**–finally, finish by lightly applying a layer of white pencil over the skin to lighten and soften it. Redefine the features and darken any shadows that need more contrast. Pick out highlights in the eyes and hair. Darken the background to allow the face to stand out.